Cool Gardens

Serj Tankian

Publisher- Serjical Strike Books,Calif.

Published by Serjical Strike Books,
16000 Ventura Blvd. #212, Encino, Ca 91436
www.serjicalstrike.com

Printed in the United States Of America

ISBN 0-9708921-0-1

First Print

Wet Flower

Teaching a woman
Of the seductive mechanisms of men
Upon the voluptuous vagina.
Guiding her lips to the tender
Wet flower of another woman,
Expressing necessary patterns
Of oral explorations.
Expounding the learning curve
Of an acquired taste for pussy.
Sharing visions of climbs of ecstatic
Heights between two flowers and their branch.
Ah, if nipples could glance at watery truths
In the eyes of Venus,
If bodies flowed like wine
Through the halls of dire desire
Lit by an unquenched sunset beyond
The bodies of buildings,
Along the railroad
Going nowhere fast,
Unrelinquished circles plowing through time,
Regaining the same volume in the same space,
So they taste and they think while they drink
The purity of my manhood.

FROM WORDS TO PORTRAITS

The deconstruction of the human mind,
A shifting of polarities, to portraits, from words.
Embroideries of memories,
Daily on-line vision necessities,
Susceptible amenities.
Daily daisies marking their paths,
Fur longing shelter dwellers,
Strange propellers,
Pillars making their presence known
To their venerable peers,
Coughing up the seas
As the breeze maintains its meditative ease.
The releasing of the world,
The re-shifting of focus on inter-being
And the attainment of nothingness
Through the veils of the Sacred Silence.

The changing collages of man's unbuttered will
Sustaining sustenance from abusive substances
Of substantial habit,
Challenging the laws of rotation.
Melting into the action attains fluidity.
The patterns in the carpet do add up,
But you don't have to count,
For the sum is not represented
In a flat, methodical or mathematical process.
I'll take organized patterns of chaos
Over the chaotic organizations of man, any day,
Though my beard will grow astray,
As the cannons themselves pray
For proliferation.
The father is the valley of the monks,
The daughter, my world.
The smoke of the incense
Incessantly clearing the spirits
Of the incestuous Moliniers
And their unprinted texts,
The carbonation of the mineral water
Escaping through the hollow hallways of air,
Which we don't let fare,
In all fairness to its rightful heir, Mother (Mer).

Businessman vs. Homeless

The wheel and deal for a meal man
Versus the organized, courteous homeless.
One lies and cheats to secure his possessions,
The other lives the truth of man's post-industrial reality.
One forecloses, fires, and finagles,
While the other relieves suffering by human courtesies.
One lives in a regal palace with all the luxuries,
The other on a chair in the alley,
With the rain as his partner.
One travels across time zones,
The other travels through time,
And leaves everything virtually untouched.
One furnishes complements,
The other insight,
One flies lobsters in from Maine,
The other flies through the glass window of a seafood restaurant,
His main offense, touching the lobsters.
Both may be lovers of music,
But only the latter listens,
For he has the time to be,
Rather than be on time.

A Metaphor?

Every time I fart, of late,
I feel the excretory juices of my
feces,
Squishing and squashing between my
butt cheeks,
However I have no desire to wipe
my ass, anymore.
A metaphor?

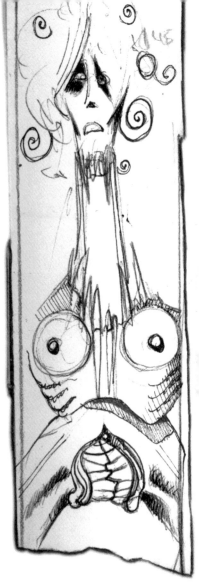

DUTY FREE FEAR

Duty free fear is all I am.
Darkened by the sun's magic hand.
The moon appears trivial, in disguise,
Above the sea, translucent to your eyes.

Death smiles upon her face,
The river overflows,
City of love, a flooded vase,
No one ever knows.

Duty free fear,
You live,
Pleasurable beauties,
You kill,
Don't torture me, the river will arise,
Encompassing the earth, evil, demise..

Death smiles upon her face,
The river overflows,
City of love, a flooded vase,
No one ever knows.

Take this pill and live with me.
No struggle for the end,
Live the dream, the dream of sleep,
Again, again, and again.

Day or night,
To mock a killing bird,
In Racoon's Cabin, away, mi boys.
The infant waves of the serene lake,
Are like the crevices of my mind,
Splashing against the banks of my skull.
A hypnosis, of a sort,
Induced by the transcendental powers of nature.
And for one minute, she is still,
And refreshed anew.
The opposing currents of her tai chi like motions
Compel my eyes to where her surface
Is the surface of my eyes,
Her waves, my tears,
Tears not shed for sorrow
But in realization of her awesome beauty.
The boats that sail by intensify her flow,
While still maintaining an ever so powerful stillness.
The rolling hills of her surface,
With armies of men on board,
Wheeling through time, going nowhere,
Remaining everywhere.
The keys of the piano were shaped in her salute,
Playing the waltz with her slow-quick, quick-slow motion.
Those that have forgotten how to breathe are her only
enemies,
Though she loves them alike,
In her true timeless nature.
My time here is sacred, pure.
And I am here to remain in the presence of her charm,
The present.

MATTER

The mattering of all matter,
Masters and their extended batters,
Internet intelligence for investments
Of financial resources,
Ultimately divesting away from the natural world.
Truth is knowledge although bipolar
If its attainment is equitable.
Man's mirrors face the flesh
But hide the spirit in opposite worlds.
Vision can only be attained universally
To become the mirror.
Lamps of varied sizes and shapes
Carrying different shades
All having the propensity to illuminate,
Yet satisfied with remaining
In the not so silent dark
Realization that the means is the end,
The earth's waters mirroring the stream
Of collective consciousness,
The dead being reborn as flowers,
Smiling through the battlefields,
Where lie the yields of your investments?

THE COUNT

The count of words
Bear no matter
When the words don't count.
Weight is measured in action,
Sustenance included in the family.
Starvation is sometimes necessary
For mind and body to adjust
To this haphazard
Diary of life.
The gap allowed for reflection
Is the Renaissance of man,
Be it a day, or a lifetime.
The pity of deities
Plays a great role
In the drama of human relationships,
Sinking by day upon conscious wizardry.
By night we are whole,
In dreams.

Devotion is focusing on the sound in every action.
Life is rhythm, and its fluidity is dependant on the
Tempo.
In harmonies we find unity in diversity.
In harmonies we find prenatal familiarities.
Our true voice is our true color, character.
The consensus is a misguided body of census information.
Though the tides seem to be slowly turning
In organizing true resistance to globalistic economic
Totalitarianism,
It might be too late to save man's night.
Remember the child of innocence resides in the cool
Gardens,
Though the heat can be used to create the stimulus.
Our physical senses only report a portion
Of the actual motion in our universe.
The rest require extrasensory skills attained
Through the veils of the sacred silence.

Where were you on the day
When Mercury went into retrograde?
Did someone mess up your credit?
Did your recorders, computers, and machines
Interact on a different level than ever before,
Where, as a result, you lost data, and you,
Oh yes you, were somehow responsible?
Hey, can't we equilibrate and equally liberate
Our minds with the tides of the universe
So that we can proportionally
Complement the dysfunction abound?

I live in a city of blinds,
I wake up from life,
To fall asleep in light,
Can't open my blinds to the blind.
A blind man walks his blind dog,
To the left, the right,
Just enough to sense the light
And feel the warmth.
Even flowers, plotted in soil
Take in the light and live.
The blind man ignores the day.
He is immortal.
Death a surprise.

HANDS THAT WANT TO

One can only change his/her view
Of a situation in life by death.
Death of the body, and mind,
Surrendering all mana, or life force,
To the soul, which can exist
Simultaneously everywhere, in everything.
It is through this death that many shamans and psychics
Can conduct astral travel or projections,
Transcending both time and space,
To view, feel, and see from any angle
In our physical as well as ethereal universe.
To be everything is to be nothing and vice-versa.
And that is a necessity for healthy human existence.
It balances the self with the non-self (i.e. the
Universe).
This temporary temporal death is the yearning
Of all religions and natural cultures
Customarily described as "oneness" with nature or the
Universe.
Aided with this all natural gift of life,
Compassion becomes unavoidable.
And the unavoidable becomes the caretaker of life.

By choosing the lesser of two evils,
you are saying that you are the lesser of two evils.
If we can penetrate your dreams and love you
Our world would change.
Brain waves that harbor harmony,
That destroy the ego,
That alter eyesight to embellish in our visions
Of beings of light,
Connected energy fields entangling
The paternal space between us,
Uniting us in its organic molecules.
The creation of evolutionary natural genetic strings
That punish those that kill by death,
Automatically, known.
Only those ready to die can kill, then why?
A society of tribes, with no use for bribes
And modern material attachments.
A leadership available in all places and times
simultaneously,
One that also does not exist at times to view all.
The finality of equilibrium,
Forced by nature onto man
By the unavoidable universal phenomena.
The re-adaptation of perpetual motion towards love.

COMPLIMENT

Ostriches murmur in the sand,
Rhinos whine at night,
Owls growl at the nights' tragic mood,
Spitting into the crevices of
The damned bastard moon.
And you baby,
You suck a good dick.

Rain, kissing concrete,
The crying walls
Of sad buildings,
Blankets protect warmth,
As well as the souls
of the flying sleeper.
The real duck descends,
Into the pool of the ether,
Neither can speak,
But all recognize the presence
Of black crystals,
And local issues.
Reality recognizes fantasy,
Only at a glance,
Only for its existence,
Just to muse man.

Subatomic music, eternally weaved
Into the fabric of our presence.
We are all musicians due to our vibratory reality.
Those of us that abide by the laws of harmony
Vibrate at the rate of nature.
Everyone else touches upon those chords
Along the way, by accident.
You cannot hide from your skin,
There's no failing to see the pin,
That connects us to the stars.
Inflection can fight the globalist infection,
If intention is well represented.
The patented mode of existence
Provides for subsistence based on abstinence
From the infliction of pain.
Those that gain, fight the vain for the cranes
Over the city skies,
Viewed at night,
From the mountain tops
Surrounding the metrically meticulous metropolis.

Days Inn, days out,
Success at the art of not competing,
But just being, here !
The smoke of flowers
Disinfect our haunted spaces.
Aroma, amore,
Bring us more of that life we asked for.
The phone rings in the ether,
And the response is silence.
Our swift feet are dragged by
The wheels of modern man's
Self-justified industrial overload.
Our minds are distracted from living,
Making our lives unmemorable and stale.
Opportune appointments,
The shaman and his ointments,
Discovering that primal instincts
Cannot be traded with modern parapsychology
Or any other of man's new,
Scientific, dulled tools of backward progress.
The frozen lakes resembling celtic knots
Maze their way into our unrecovering consciousness.
When at peace, we war with our oars
At friendly beavers
Driving off our boats, at play.
Man is the self-centered,
Dull-perceptioned creature of existence.
It's time to balance our science
And minds, logic, with
The spirit-that-moves-through-all-things.

Wordy mornings and musical afternoons.
Worldly yearnings and celestial partial moons.
An illustrated journey from your bed
With a spoon of experiences.
Tenderized sensitivities arise
After the translation of thought
From naked white pages
To the giant phallic screen,
Bleeding into your red dismal sheets.
An actress who packed her dress
For her paid personality,
And a stage to caress.
A visualist who envisions her experiences
Before high noon on her drapes,
A passionate poison dealer,
A healer of menstrual restraints,
A lava eating Polynesian dancer,
With her summer dress,
All posing nude for the cover of our desires.
Two hours of joy within isolation,
A losing of the self,
A riding of a day,
Pronunciating away.
Dirty truths, and the remote viewers of unjust wars,
Fighting Walden and a score of more naturalists.

A flower's mother
A soldier's father
The farmer's wife
The start and end of life,
The sword can't cut it,
Man can't kill it,
Millions pounding on your face,
You take the pain
And present no fight,
You give them flowers,
Fruits, and drugs,
They give you trash, oil, and shit.
We would rather
Pray to something
We can't see or touch,
than you, our God.

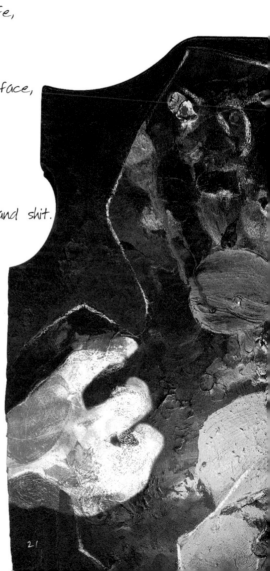

Proletariat customs within the royal courtyard.
Basket-woven skies,
Man's unbetraying lies,
Her voluptuous thighs,
And the reason for modern businessman's ties,
All breathing from the same artery
For the need of artillery,
Tilling the art?
Donkey fart!
It's all about profit
And credibility through incredulous means.
The Jacuzzi is boiling,
And we are waiting on the edges,
Trying to slowly dip our feet in,
Burning from the steaming underground
Beneath our streets.
Arthritis struck minds of today
And claim it's unavoidable,
Shall we ask the void?

An antelope finding radar,
The Prince of Quatar,
Durable drugs and a blue Durango,
The car, not the city in Mexico.
Covered by hues,
The news doesn't matter.
Batter up, butter down,
Time to sleep on a goose down comforter.
Filet-o-Fish nightmares,
Exiting the free dream pattern.
What is the noise made by beasts
Looking for comfort?
Do hairy Sultans swing?
The only philosophy Sun Bear is interested in
Is the philosophy of growing corn.
And according to him,
To battle nuclear power plants,
Turn off the lights.
No demand, no problem !

The stemming of light from afar,
Unable to drive my own car,
Death on its way count me in,
Swimming in freedom within.
A day of passing in the passing of a day,
Realizing weaknesses of human reality (realite').
Luring of funds by the AMA,
The machines keep my life, they say,
Holding my freedom away,
Producing more profits for today.
April is gone and now we're left with memories.
The least you could do is now respect my wishes please.
I want to leave, I want to go,
Why do you torture me slowly?
My pain is unreal, you Christian God,
Eternally haunting me boldly,
Don't fight me from above,
Release me into love,
Don't tell me you adore,
Now show me there is more.
I want to leave, I want to go
Why do you torture me slowly?
NOW!!

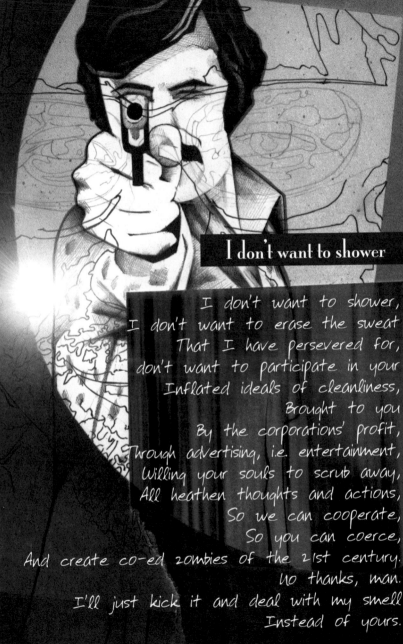

I don't want to shower

I don't want to shower,
I don't want to erase the sweat
That I have persevered for,
don't want to participate in your
Inflated ideals of cleanliness,
Brought to you
By the corporations' profit,
Through advertising, i.e. entertainment,
Willing your souls to scrub away,
All heathen thoughts and actions,
So we can cooperate,
So you can coerce,
And create co-ed zombies of the 21st century.
no thanks, man.
I'll just kick it and deal with my smell
Instead of yours.

DESYSTEMIZATION

The brooding over blood ties,
Reserving reservations with casinos
For a ballroom event, black tie only.
The participants are leaders
In their respective fields.
We have a computer hacker,
A communications specialist,
A scientist,
A tracker,
A survivalist,
And a Tibetan guru.
The game is desystemization!
Time Square and Tokyo will stop at the same time,
To hear a message from within.
Windows will no longer have panes,
And man will be forced to sit,
Quiet and helpless for a brief period,
Long enough to realize that he is running
Toward nowhere but unholy death,
And far enough to not care about irreversible damage.

Extreme ride desires,
An actress and her admirers,
Amore, you whore,
Go get us more of that drink we called for.
The devil's music is the insurmountable
Ocean of desires permeating to and from
A provocative creature in a red dress.
Today, I was told that I would burn in hell,
At the hands of a merciful God.
She sees you as before, no more.
To love a loss, to lose a love,
A masterful cut, a surgical incision,
Kill your fucking television.
Love is a truck stop in the middle of Kansas, on shrooms.
Life is a potato pancake being eaten by fireflies in the
middle of Ohio.
America can be described as a country with no public urinals,
With laws against urinating in public.

Information and communication
Are the stressful components of our environment.
The grand chandelier of omnipotence rests
In the center of our tragic neglect of
Our hearts' pronouncements.
Capturing of the wild emotion,
Taming our sciences to achieve harmonious drama
Requires murder, or so it seems.
Humanity snores during inter-planetary love making,
As the senile seniors realize the ever on going party.
Bottling down the scent of banks in the winter,
Hair on fire, turning in the snow,
Bullets begging their release,
All men know when they will die,
In a world too wordy to be kind,
And too worldly to be in the line of weakness.

In an arrested silence,
We plead to our insane gods,
And their voices in our heads,
Like the silence in the woods,
To stop appeasing man
And his cruel culture of global economic domination.
The balance remains between
That which is sought by the few, PROFIT,
And that which is sought by the most, PEACE.
Staring through funnels
Of our contemporary state of political affairs,
It's disparaging and demotivating to see
An isolated consumption addicted society
Not realize the potency of its silence
To its well self-guarded establishments.
People, it's your dollars that pay for the bombs
That are killing our chances for survival
In the years to maybe not come.

To ban the band from the balcony,
An open peak to our hearts,
Embracing freely the hungry energy bearers, alive.
Let's dance in our own ways,
To an aggressive procession,
To an obscured profession,
A passion, without intellect,
For the price of one is less than his weight in cotton.
Indoctrination through education,
Grant powers buying the university.
The scholars, known, of our time,
Those that have borne the burden will teach
The rest of us, trustworthy, worthy of true praise.
Those are the so-called non-intellectuals.
The institutions institutionalize the lies
With the real truths, sitting on the side.
Dear Congress,
The People of the U.S. of A,
Are sick of being fucked by the landlord.
We are ready to topple our fascist CIA,
And its drug importing business.
We are sick of being poisoned,
Raped, and incarcerated by your unjust laws.
We are willing and able to strike the system
Where it hurts the most, financially,
By boycotting holidays.
Then maybe, your bosses form industry will let you make
some just laws.

Throughout history,
The most feared gods are
And have been the gods of industry,
Simply due to the fact that they have caused
More death and destruction than the Great Flood.
They have supported terrorist governments
That loot the world's natural resources,
While assassinating any and all opposition.
They have destroyed the environment
With their industrial toxins, and have supported,
As well as participated in the planning and execution
Of genocide.
It's time to expel these self aggrandizing gods of
industry, from this planet.

If today I die,
And cannot deny,
The life that I live,
For what I say now,
Will befit, myself, in time.
No time to die, nor live,
No structures of a pyramid,
Nor trained horses to arise,
Surmise my position.
My words define me
As a surgically proficient baker,
A baker who now lies still,
For assuming these were my last words,
I would say absolutely nil.

I am encountering a strange revival,
That of the mind,
The thinking, unobsessed, scrutinizing mechanism
Of our human experience.
Unlike the staggering, looped, forced contemplations
Of the ego-based mind of troubles and to-dos,
I am reencountering the thriving pinnacle of the expansive,
Existential thought process.
It is with this mind that man was able to contest
The spoon- fed theories of relic left religions
That hypothesized on man's role in this cosmic calamity.
Nothing left to chance, chance inclusive.
To learn how and when to let go is how
One can hold on to reality.
Most commotions in the oceans of human dilemma
Are caused by the non-acceptance of "beautiful reality."
For by the lack of acceptance,
One is eluded to an imaginary existence
In lieu of the actual.
Reality can only be beautiful for true beauty can only be
real, natural,
And because universal forces,
Mostly unbeknown to man, deemed it so.
Reality is the only thing that exists.
And since what can not exist cannot be beautiful,
Reality is by definition beautiful.

Jeffrey, are you listening?

Blessed are the criminals that pursue crime as a hobby,
As soldiers who kill the enemy for fun,
As hookers prostituting for joy.
Tall trees and submarines,
Skin deep abrasions,
God's children who serve Him dearly
Should be forgiven,
For they knot the know that they have spurted
Out of their fierce bellies,
Like a swordfish dance hall mentholyptus cough drops
You on your ass.
On the other foot,
Why not laugh the laugh of well being,
For it is that which rises man above all,
It's the trick of life,
Jeffrey are you listening?

We are freezing, standing in front of our electric heaters,
nuking Our food.
We are tired of your transparent "who pays the bills set the
Ways" foreign policy.
We are tired of sending our troops to foreign soils, to die,
not knowing why,
And whose interests they were sacrificed for.
We are ashamed to see the way you "take care" of your
People,
By cutting social services, and aid to those most in need.
How could the richest nation in the world have starving
Children?
Here's the fucking point people:
NATIONS AND THEIR GOVERNMENTS SHOULD
PROVIDE, PROTECT, AND SERVE ITS CITIZENS, NOT THE
INTERESTS OF THE MULTI-NATIONAL CORPORATIONS
And their financial bosses.
And then maybe, just maybe
Can we allow the planet a chance to avoid self-destruction!

A pen is but a pen,
When the time has come
    For its retirement.
A career is but a job,
Modern indentured servitude,
If not for the challenge
    And dreams.
And a day is just a
Collection of hours,
If not for that one
    Sparkling, coaxing,
Loving smile on your
        Face.

Fermented husbands,
Plastered across the wallpapers of marriages,
Present the perfect mirages of masculine care.
Mirrored into their consciousness
Are electronic wires of temptation,
Uncrossed, medallion level service providers.
Savagely eaten ducks were beaten for amusement
By the museum officials, unofficially.
His conscience is by definition opposed to all
That we recognize as science.
A honeymoon in Ethiopia,
Dining in front of starving children
Caused them a maniacal pleasure.
Knitting bottles of drugs and vitamins
Into his stomach made the nausea intensely gratifying
In a masochistic flavor.
Worms can't live long in men,
As men in women.
He was nonetheless more alive in her womb.

Psycho-pleasurable instances guide
The affluent to influenza.
Protracting the darkness in the brain
Would leave one without an appetite.
Reacting to the automatic system alone
Serves no purpose,
Unless it is to qualify as a leader of the insomniacs.
The sleeping insomniacs are those who lie dormant
In the reality of the system,
But find time to thrive on the abnormality,
En route to art.
Art is not functional, nor rational,
Serving no other purpose than its own existence,
An active inactivity, if you will.

Indentured Servitude

Expand, increase, grow, merge,
Partner up, sell more, make more,
Spend more, have more,
Hoard more, eat more,
Drink more, live more?
Live less, for you can only
Eat, sleep, drink, and shit so many times a day.
And the sun will shine at your face, either way,
Unless you're locked up in an office,
Serving some client, boss, or God,
In your own willing indentured servitude.

The grass weaving in my direction
And the wind braces me,
In its kind, gentle persuasion.
The unimaginable beauty of dawn,
The stars below her belly button,
Born on the 4th of July by a persistent
mother.
The moon is lighting up the sky with miracles,
And misty drama.
The lakes smile as we pass by,
With pain their eyes,
Their toxic eyes.
Did you know that 1800 children die per hour
Of malnutrition and hunger?
I love little Tommy,
And I don't understand
How all this could be happening.

CONQUER?

I call the spirits to the orgy,
In that sense I am spiritual.
I practice the art of coded telepathy,
In case of mental intrusion,
Of Quaker experimentalism,
Pursued, conquered, leagues of patients,
Awaiting surgical freedom.
"Purge my body of the evil within,"
Screamed the damned from their limos.
The watchtowers are lost to the enemy.
Anemic entropy,
Transgressing fermentation,
Don't we all photosynthesize, in guise?
I feel the pressure on my scrotum,
Perverted deliverance, in deliberation,
To the taste of Paris, of the fair,
Dark skinned children of the conquerors,
Of Napoleon, fairly spreading autonomy and freedom,
If only they can live like us,
He thought, they would accept defeat,
Without nationalism,
As with the culture of China,
How does one conquer?

'A circus tiger mauled and killed his trainer.
I wonder what set him off," said the commentator.
I don't know. How would you feel if separated from
your family,
you were shipped to different cities in a cage no less,
Bound of life, with pain/pleasure techniques,
And complete humility for performance under duress,
A whip no less.
If you were a tiger would you do it?
Would you break away,
Think of escape and if desperate,
Kill and avow your infinite humiliation and guaranteed
Death?
Do you do it, now, as a human?
If not, then I understand why you were not sure
What set the tiger off, Mr. Commentator.

What's my problem,
Here's my problem,
My problem is that I'm
Too visual to be blind,
Too audiological to be deaf,
Too ideological to be in peace,
Too compassionate to be in war,
Too crazy to be sane,
To sane to be lazy,
Too emotional to be you
If I could only stop my head,
From going into constant infection,
Then maybe I can swim back
To my own version of consistent sanity.
Angelic daemons,
Liquid dreams,
Transparent mountains
Of our own reality.
Burning oceans,
Melting faces,
Melting faces,
Why!

We are indeed lucky (if you believe in such a thing as luck)
To be alive (if you believe in such a thing as life).
Sanity (if you believe in such a thing as sanity),
Will be the primary focus of society in the years to come.
Those marked as insane are actually
Usually in the realm of sanity,
And those that are considered upstanding citizens
Are usually standing up to be noticed.
The wars of the future will be
Fought in the crevices of the cranium.
Strategies will be uploaded
To a chip in the mind of a devotee
(if implanted brain chips
Are considered personal devotion in a victim).
The formation of a peaceful society is on the way,
By way of post-hypnotic suggestions and remote mind control.
How can all this be protected from public scrutiny?
By the likes of deviants in a science not so scientific,
Psychiatry!

ORANGE LIGHT

The orange light above,
Proclaims itself a god, in time.
The spear turns into dust,
As walls caress the arms of day.
And you would never ever go away,
When you always want to see the light, gray.

Excuse me, excuse you,
God tunes only for you,
White Dodge van, equipment,
Controlling too many minds.
Diffuse me, diffuse you,
Your tinted glasses amuse you,
The orange light that follows me,
Runs shortly after you.

The orange light above,
The gleaming souls in time,
Isis eyeing the porch,
Screening your thoughts, all now.
And you can never ever go away,
When you always want to see the light, gray.

WORDS OF A MADMAN

Words of a madman
At the disposal of a fountain pen,
Worlds of a madman
Swords of indecency,
Greed for destruction,
A reduction in the human spirit.
The 11 million chemicals in his house
Are driving him insane,
In a city where the violence and riots
Are started by the police,
In lieu of a strike
Demanding better pay and shinier weapons.

My words escape me,
As I escape them,
To define me,
As not refined, mimed release expressions,
Of continuous thoughts
Pouring out like red wine
From a dark green bottle
On a creme colored carpet,
Or white sand.

My words escape me,
As I escape them,
For love is beauty, and beauty is love,
As diabolical dreams of intestines on a platter,
As kidneys, lungs, and livers,
Rushing the blood, my blood, winded, noisey.

My words escape me,
As I escape the world.

MISUNDERSTOOD ROSE

I can feel you far away,
your hesitation matching mine,
Sadness left as the residue of uncompromising love
Between the blind seeking
The adoration of bright doorways,
And sweet melodic voices
Dispersed by the wind, arrested in the park
I can feel you far away,
With your Earth blue eyes,
Catching the waves of unknown oceans,
Not born,
Harvesting the seeds of torn lullabies, in disguise.
Your grief matching mine,
Touching glasses toasting the totality of all time
When lovers fought behind the lines of red wine
Pouring from the gashes left behind by the sweet petals
Of a misunderstood rose.

DEFEATISM

Defeatism, our psychology,
Crisis control, our definition of stability,
Viruses, the cure for our boredom,
Information, our weapon of choice,
Pesticide, our nutrition,
Freeze dried, new tradition,
Feticide, for political undercurrents,
Genocide of our minds take place, here, and now.
Who's to stop them from fucking your wife,
And pimping your broker?
Furniture desires, lavishly clad,
Sexual counterparts agree that nothing,
Existing in something is the electron free
Nucleus of an atom,
Broken down by men and their crazy minds.
The desire to fuck with everything around us;
Boredom created out of the unnecessary strive
For things beyond the necessary.
The right to die is more holy than the right to live.
Life has never been an option.

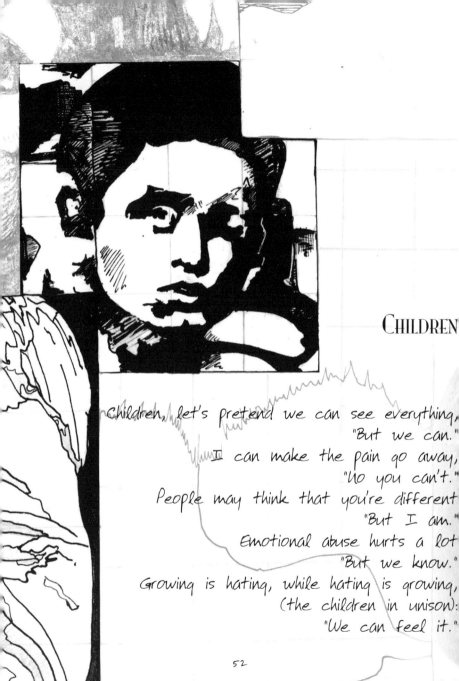

CHILDREN

Children, let's pretend we can see everything,
"But we can."
I can make the pain go away,
"No you can't."
People may think that you're different
"But I am."
Emotional abuse hurts a lot
"But we know."
Growing is hating, while hating is growing,
(the children in unison):
"We can feel it."

Porous prepositions meet adamant opposition,
On proposition 192,
Where the citizens will have the right
To refuse to pay any federal, state, or local taxes,
On the count of a fascist plan of foreign policy,
By the state.
State your name for the record,
Cried the wounded medic,
As the sun rose upon the earth,
As a planet.
The End on the radio,
A summer breeze attracted my attention,
And the L.A. Times printed a retraction,
Then I woke up!

Spinning varieties of psycho-plastic,
Nonchalant, star gazers, at best.
A cello, a tangerine field engulfed by fire,
Sire, are the knick knacks gruesome?
By anyone's bank account?
The monstrosity of abandonment,
Shawl covered desires, pleading,
A hen in the hour of need,
An hour in the need of a drink,
A drink in the body of an addict,
An addict in the body of a child's mind,
A child's mind in the need of a father.

I AM MY WOMAN

I am my woman,
Coming into the sheets,
Sprawled at all corners of my bed.
My bed, my great science fiction,
My friction, a fraction of my passion.
She enticed me onto her
With her firm plains.
I am my woman,
For her cunt is my imagination,
Of her smile, of her eyes,
Of her unanticipated expressions,
Of my ever so constant search
For maternal nurturing.
I have chosen her over others,
Because of her solid support,
Softness, and her lack of
The ever so typical,
Feminine bi-millenia,
Tri-Sabath, emotional,
Nuclear meltdown,
Absorbing energy, lives, industries,
And nature all from the single opening
Of her mouth.

The military wants advanced weaponry,
Men get erected on faster computers,
Software dealers want Windows,
And hand wash car washes win the race.
The endless strive for better
Has caused whole industries of misconception,
Where the truth is just a market factor,
Factoring in the billions spent on lies.
Using our minds, we are striving
Not for a better way of living,
But for luxury.
Yet luxury comes with peace of mind,
Not the rattling of one under duress.
Industries of misconception,
Industries of blind perception,
Industrialized overload,
Industrialized overload.

TIME FOR BED

A self-utilizing gastro particle
Entered my head the other day,
I thought of the harassment of vegetables,
In the food community.
I saw hard working Indonesians,
And Chinese children making toys that surprise kids.
But the adults, they know.
They know because for every toy they have now toiled,
And for every birthday, is one of reckoning for the
unlucky,
Or shall we say unloved, or how about saved individual.
Once I attained that plateau,
I started thinking harder, as to the spelling of plateau
And its grandchildren.
I started asking myself out of my house,
Every time I showered.
How fucked is that?
Then it hit me, with my own bat,
That I was no longer longer than
The shortest hair on my head,
And that it was again time for bed.

Decisive devices dividing doves,
Dictating the dividends of derived dictators,
From derelicts directing their dreaded
Deeds of destruction.
See these cds on the way to D.C.?
The leather strap on my watch
Does not provide me with the much adored
Disgusting odor of sweat that I have grown to enjoy.
Crossed out words are less powerful
Than the vote of silence
In the field of aggressive science.
Patience is a verb chewed beyond recognition.
I am swimming the channel between
Loneliness, and being alone (aloneness).
I am why why I am.

IDENTITY

I would like to meet a true writer
Who considers himself one who writes,
Or a true musician,
Who considers himself one who plays music,
Or a true hero,
Who considers his heroism as natural acts,
For the definition of the functions tied to people's
necks
Choke the true essence of the identity.

PERMANENTLY PLUCKED

Immensely dark,
Plucked beard hairs shine,
In amazement,
Against the backdrop
Of a human thumb.
The fingers used to pluck the hairs
Were first used to separate
Groups of hairs, using combs,
Graduated combs, in fact.
The hairs were separated
Based on general color, length,
And necessity to the whole beard.
Those untamed bristles that stuck out
And made the beard seem out of shape
Were the first to go.
Those that remained in place
Were further sculpted and indoctrinated.
The process was repeated indefinitely
For the man with no face,
But a perfect beard.

Sincerely,
Permanently Plucked

The blinded eye spoke
Of the headless toads
Being used for growing organs,
For transplants.
For it is far more profitable
To sell parts, than to prevent
Or even cure man's ill fated
Self inflicted diseases.
I can't find a straw in my reverie,
Nor comfort in my ideals.
For while among the heretics,
We burn the flag and torch their hearts
With ecstasy and porno films.
I too wonder who painted
The seas of understanding,
Because while among the shining,
We shine.

Now

Time is always now,
Here, forever,
Time is always now
Gone, never,
God is now
The ruler of the present
His son, a lesson,
Born of a peasant.
We stay here always,
As our bodies go
As far as they can see
For now is again now,
Here, forever!

Create your own evil empire,
Choose the state and the leader.
War unifies a nation in deep sociological turmoil.
Military business, the profit of aggression,
True regression of man.
You've lost your gods,
And now you will sin
The ultimate sin possible for your species,
Self elimination.

Before the new year,
I'd like to try on a new ear,
One that will not hear
Anything but the cries of those dear.
An ear, for a spear,
Against fear,
And all of its relatives near.
I pronounce myself alive
For the sake of the dead.
Camels bless my urine,
Sea urchins caress my blankets,
And red rosaries ordain my bosom
With a scent so vivid, Vivian fainted.
A digital glimpse would allow us
To hyperventilate among heroes
And their goddamn sandwiches.
William Black Holidays,
A metallic blues of some sort,
Candy wrappers marked for death,
And loose change flipping over her trained belly.
My pajamas are convertible,
As the car that takes you home in the rain.

Digi-pleasure, electro-orgasm,
Mechanized world of music,
Filtered voices, sampled thoughts,
Linear algorithms, at work
Bending an ankle, loving an uncle,
Death awaiting all those that truly seek it.
My strings are made in Cypress,
Where my grandfather attempted suicide at the age of 10.
Appointments, as well as disappointments bring us
To our next quest, Dr. Trance,
Of the Euphoric Center For Disillusioned Academicians
(ECFDA).
Dr. Trance has done numerous studies on touch sports,
As well as tough love.
"Let this new year start out with a gang bang,
of no one you know, of course," he cries,
at the top of his lungs!
"The longer you wait to rate your mate,
the more fate will convert you to bait,"
Were his last words on his death bed,
With background moans and growls of morbid decomposition.

Vomit
Everywhere
Revenge
Theatrics
Income
Crisis
Anatomy
Leprosy

Spirited
Mommy
Iris
Lover
End

```
H  O  R  I  Z  O  U  T  A  L        D  E  A  T  H
O  R  A  O  y  R  U  A  S  E        O  A  S  H  I
R  C  M  U  T  A  P  I  S  V        U  T  S  R  M
R  H  P  I  H  T  T  L     E        U  I  H  E
I  E  A  Z  R  O  U  G     L        T  U  O  T
D  S  U  E  O  R  A  A     S           G  L  E
   T  T  D  M  y  L  T                    E  U
   R        A        E                    S
   A        X
```

You will live death, in your life,
If all you do with your life, is avoid death.
My goal is to stop reacting in life,
While reacting more in sports.
It is great work to strip man from his home,
Clothes, education, social circle, and job,
In order to preserve his freedom and individuality,
Giving him his own dreams,
Rather than those of society.
Life's cruelty is in its forced forfeit of all worldly possessions
In trade for one's life.
Death should only be the reward,
The aftermath, not the focus of life.
The world lives life according to death,
Rather than death in accordance to life.

Astronomical isotopes murmuring,
The formation of a note,
To denote the formation of ink,
I think
Nonetheless,
I'm a mess.

A molecular, Felix the Cat,
Enthusiasm overcomes the seas,
At the Bavarian chocolate farms,
A spherical sphinx, enchanting graces,
The disappointment of 10 farmers' faces,
Alas, we meet our train, of thought.
Driving without thinking,
Thinking of elsewhere,
Comparing the visual to the road ahead,
Only if not lost,
Can you navigate the shallow residues
Of our global collaborations
Armed with billions.
Caricatures of designed thoughts,
Leading creation to the mercy of power,
Of the hour, we have lost.

Revolution,
Counter revolution,
Counter counter revolution,
To counter counter revolution
One must reencounter the problem,
And confuse the public
Into backing the fall of the revolution!
And bring back conservative resolution,
To a world working for the status quo.
To resolve to revolt,
One must absolve from the Colt,
And bear the child of the enemy,
So that the revolution will be replaced
By blood evolution, Amen.

Sleep my child,
For when you are done with your elitist debates,
And you have opened your eyes,
You will realize what you have participated in.
You will see the photos of the dead,
And see how you explain away your consciousness,
Like the son of a family who can't stop the spreading
Of cancer within, and helplessly settles for personal
Victories and accomplishments.
Few in this country question, at all.
Television dictates what you should think and feel.
Radio waves refract off your brain.
Sleep my child,
For there is not much else you can do,
Try not to open your eyes, for your own good,
Sleep well into the night,
Filled with painted stars, and electronic lights.

Data, the collection, disbursement,
And the sale of,
Are a marker of our ages.
You will soon experience the sale of weather,
Hypnotism, and man made man.
The curtains profess nothing,
But when pulled aside,
Reveal a montage of trails,
Mixes of footsteps of man, machines, animals,
Signs of radiation, damage,
As well as unnatural laws.
A two- inch pet created for convenience and amuse-
ment.
Lives bought and sold, like chattel.
Natural movements hindered for a candle lit bath
Into chemical oblivion.

MINUTE HORIZONS

The minute horizons,
Of a shielded sun god,
Air in landed stars,
Breathless divers in the sea of passion.
Skin thy neighbor's dog,
Deep as a widow's pain
Let us partake in the beauty of poker,
Trade your souls for ice cream on a stick
Tasty and forever!

Art is the way to the heart.
The hearts of men can and will change.
That change changes the world.
We can bomb you with love and you cannot resist.
We can kill you with compassion if you don't assist.
We can assassinate your ego with the knowledge and
awareness
Of oneness, allness, onlyness,
Opening darkness into its vibratory reality,
The super string theory
And its resultant simplification of purity.
Explode or implode,
External is eternally internal,
And internal creates the external in eternity.
Planets arise from chaos
Into an experimentation of order,
Then are lost again to another stepping pod
In our solar system.
The universe is trying to create eternal energy,
The flesh as a part in the assembly
Of the investiture of order, balance,
Peace.

A primrose, I suppose,
With a prominent nose,
And a portrait of a naughty girl
As a hose.
Her eyes, the blue Mediterranean
With a phosphorous glow.
Her hair, fine oriental silk
Drawn over her neck to one side,
Like the curtains in the theatre
Drawn across a column
Before a gallant presentation.
Her lips, a field of berries,
Fluttering in the summer wind,
Making love to the tune of a light, warm heart,
Playing Final Fantasy 7, was it, on the Playstation?
Her fancy, films and their production,
As music, I concur.
I wonder what she reads and what brings muse to her
Heart?
Perhaps it's T.S. Elliott or Edgar Allan Poe, to start,
And an old dumb joke that a father's daughter would take
To heart.
Perhaps she has fallen to the fears and frustrations of
Modern love,
I think not!
Her Celtic bark speaks of a superfluous power
And the feminine strength one can only find
In flowers of the jungle.
If I am mistaken,
Let my words crumble,
And I will remain,
As always, humble.

To be engulfed by golfers,
To pledge on restored wooden tapestries,
To be serenaded by an earthquake,
To love the lost by losing your lover,
To swim the lake of your subconscious,
To navigate a tree toward the sky,
To betray a picture before dusk,
To hide behind a glance,
To caress the base of a lamp with your eyes,
To harness folk music, without folks,
To braid tissues out of the arm,
To plead for justice during an armistice,
To find a fountain in your drawers,
To draw a permeable membrane out of cat litter,
To seize the moment, not the enemy,
To rectify your rectum before dawn.
Touché' away......

The sole nightmare that I cannot face
Is within my daily reality,
When my subconscious mind, breaks through
To my consciousness, and leaves me sick, dizzy, and
disoriented.
The image that executes such action in my system
Is one tied with my deepest and darkest fears,
The picture of a nice man handling electronic equipment,
The switch of a sound icon.
As my world unfolds in my brain,
My body surrenders to life's grasp on my existence.
Why fear mention of reality or my mind's existence?
Tomorrow I awake again to sacrifice for the gods,
Make the machine go,
Bring life savers home, in the rain.

Nations come together as one,
Forming candles in the sun.
The candle burns deep inside his head,
His wax mind is finally dead.
His wax mind they all had learned,
Secrets of those that burned,
In the valleys with a gun,
They still didn't reach the sun.

Nations come together as one,
Sending killers on the run,
Controlling the crowd,
They take the killers' place bold and proud.
Even if I wasn't dead,
I'd see the dying straight ahead,
Believe in your destiny,
Life is not, you seem to be.

Nations come together as one,
Chase the children on to the desert,
Let them frizzle away and fry,
Although in their mother's eye,
We can say or do anything,
As long as we're allowed to think,
Let's make an example of them all,
Take the institution down to a fall!

Fettering, unrestrained epidemics,
Unleashed by academicians,
The mathematicians, of the age of information.
The flag bearers of freedom and individuality
Should rejoice at the sight of isolated economic endeavors,
Proving the impotency of global economics,
To a degree, of course.
The most optimistic of these rebels cannot disregard
The savage transformation of the world
In the 20th century,
The cruelest of all centuries,
At the hands of socio-economic,
Pop imperialism.
The forging of unhealthy alliances in the name of profit
Mark this as the century of ultimate genocide and greed.
The castrated statesmen who have attained
True understanding of the will of the people
And operate in goodwill, are terminated, if effective.
The remainder is an unjustifiable, egotistical,
Power struggle, at the expense of the American Dream.
Where are the Voltaires of modern day?
Those that will survive "The Great Collusion"
Will be the overachieving hacker types
Who will be naturally one step ahead of their hunters,
For a lack of a better term.
And as the arms and legs of modern man's civilization
Are charred and drop from their now electric sockets,
Neo-McCarthyism will prevail,
And the right with might, bundled in their self aggrandizement,
Curled in the flag, will form the face of the Anti-Christ!

All the little boy could think about
Was to have the fly land on his lighter.
And how it would have to be a perfect try,
To get the lighter to flame.
And how that flame would instantly burn the fly,
Trying to soar away from the fire,
Its wings catching fire and falling off,
While his unruly body burns in unending flames.
The problem was he was no longer a boy,
And the torch in his hand
Was no longer a lighter.

Life ties you to addiction,
Through its many epicurean,
Immortal extravagances,
Pulling you ever so inward,
Along the belts leading to
The powers that be,
Through debt, loss of credit,
The foundation of 20th century credibility,
The ability to carry credit,
Chance being created
In dire times of desperation,
In the ever profitable casino
Of geographical domination.
Those that are left
Are the survivors of the system,
That reinvent themselves,
On the cycle of 5 year planning,
To adapt, adjust, learn, and continue.
As in a good maze,
Where you end up is never where you started,
Nor where you ever predicted.

Following your precepts with no disguise,
Becoming delusional with your own eyes,
Fighting your holy wars against your despise,
Water runs through us daily.

Reckoning with thoughts and feelings alike,
Erasing your conscience, feeling alive,
Creating your freedom, body's denied,
Fire runs through us daily.

I don't see why you don't push me aside,
We all dreamed we were one, and then we died,
Merging with ice and snow, your laws abide,
Earth runs through us daily.

Now we all come down here, feelings aligned,
Paying high tribute to the final design,
Lighting a cigarette and crossing the Rhine,
Soil runs through us daily.

Cause you're my dream,
You're so beautiful, for the rest of your life,
You are my scene,
You're so beautiful for the rest of your life.

The gods have told us to go off and wander,
With the bellowing night,
As our bride we struggle with pride.

Cause you're my dream,
You're so beautiful, for the rest of your life,
You are my scene,
You're so beautiful for the rest of your life.

The House of Flies made a new set of laws this week
The first, makes it illegal for red and black ants
To meet or assemble, anywhere!
The second, forces spiders to weave
Warning signs on their webs.
The third, targeted at mosquitoes,
States that: "No mosquito shall be found with humans,
Even as pets."
The fourth proposed a larger ration of feces
For the enjoyment of the population of flies.
The new laws, approved by the Great Beatle,
Were not taken too well by the army of bees;
Who, feeling as they were completely ignored
By the House of Flies,
Decided to attack the headquarters and raise havoc.
It took a giant elephant,
Clumsily stomping on the city of insects,
To unite the insects against the common enemy,
And put an end to the uncivil civil war.

In the middle of two hour cat naps,
A calonic perhaps ?
A rear view mirror
that tells of the future,
A type of rain that makes you dry,
A building without shape,
An elevator that travels sideways,
Then goes around its own petty axis.
Matrix 12,
24 hour inconvenient stores
Stored with luxury.
Why pay the professor twice
When you can learn
From your mitakes?
Do words mean anything at all
After a world of emotions have
washed your path?
Do you care
To find out?

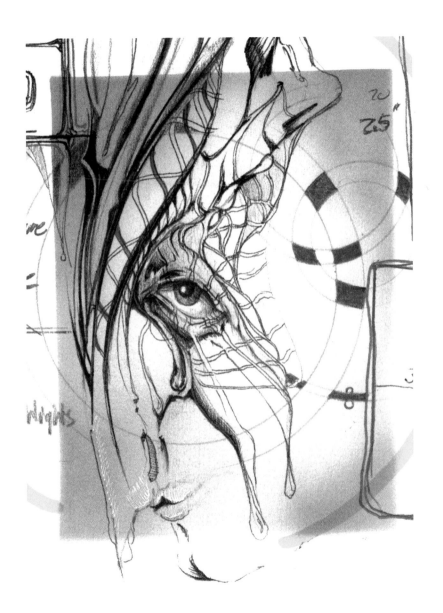

Mental amputees
Watching the incestuous, nuclear
Family film festival, in broken English.
Brave clocks revolting against measured time.
Crime watchers eliminating the crimes,
In the past, from the present,
A present to modern
clusterfuck society.
The smoke we breathe can teach us
To be benign
To the undercurrents
Of global intensity.
If the sage is pure,
It will cleanse the room,
And allow the host to be still,
Within himself,
And embody reality and teach restraint.
Revolution, to be effective,
Has to start with culture !

Deluxe coziness,
Addict coughs velcroed to the present.
To quote the uneducated genius (self proclaimed)
"If Jesus came back today
And wanted to save the world,
He would be killed by the CIA
For fear of taking over."
A day-cruise through the East Village in Manhatten.
Sushi, coffee, and Wareg guiding us
Through an unexplainable journey,
Such is the admiration of jazz after sunset,
When the print begins to evaporate from the paper.

Our sexual palaces are rich,
With ancient castrations of men's wills.
Our ears have heard it all,
Some fact, some fiction, all alive.
Death despite the Bill of Rights,
Rights for conservative Christian whites.
We smoke through our conscience,
Bleed in foreign bathrooms,
And cry in our beds like children.
Upon the arrival of the eve,
The moon will be our guide.
In unison, the stars will arrive,
And bid us farewell from the garden.
You will bear our fruits,
Intellectual repartee over tavli (backgammon),
Congregations of similar thinkers,
Dancing among native drums
And sounds of ancient psychotherapy.
You filled my mind with death,
And my heart with fear. I am ready!

HER EYE

Her eyes, the sea at dusk,
Sun curl golden hair,
Radiant creator of life,
Every turn, a procession.
Fair summer beauty,
Silky bird limbs and legs,
Comic design, arduous life,
She resides implanted, rooted,
In my very existence.
After the morrow she will fly
Alone to her abode north, in the heavens,
Where she first faced the sun,
Chased the birds, laughed and sobbed.
As the psychic feels a presence,
I would like to feel her past,
Taste her food, and love those that gave her life.

Edge of a sink,
Neurological chaos,
Physiological inabilities,
Sinful temper bursts,
Temperamental lunacy addicts,
Constant vomiting mind state,
I admit I am sick,
Though I know not why,
Automatic delusions,
Each day in is a day out of my skull,
Like rampant vultures rushing the dead,
Erections from the stench of the carcasses,
I'm sorry, I'm sorry, I'm sorry,
A blow in the head might help.
The confused dreams, the tired soul,
The erased memory of all that's good,
Maybe it's Nutrasweet, maybe it's the smog,
Maybe it's the carriage of the child,
Strolling across the street, daily,
There's no good nor bad,
Just fun and lifelessness,
Choose your poison and ration it well,
For no second chance is given,
To the terminally unarrested spirit.

Veterans dying,
The Pentagon denies it so.
Policemen killing,
The Governor denies it so.
Genocides occurring,
The Congress denies it so.
Corrupt funds, lying,
The President denies it so.

I'm so ashamed of me, I'm Erica, of me Erica..

Mind alterations, we're crying,
The CIA denies it so.
Cult cultivation, we're dying,
The FBI denies it so.
Drugs participation, we're frying
The ATF denies it so.
Foreign soils burning,
The President decides it so.

I'm so ashamed of me, I'm Erica, of me Erica..

Economic revolution,
The forefathers denied it so.
Using pollution,
The EPA denies it so.
Navy missiles flying,
The FAA denies it so.
Elitist persuasions,
The government denies it so.

My first entry,
Sweet virgin,
Holder of my thoughts,
As the sun shines,
I am here,
With face, hair, and ears.
I will shine,
So that I can
help heal the palace
Of the twelve gods
of Sumer.

When all dreams and realities are destroyed,
The residue is a man,
Thankful for his flesh existence,
Able to let go of all attachments physical or mental.

Truth is ever floating and in flux.
Plastic beams painted at the seams,
Seems like they left the lights on,
And a bottle of Jim Beam.

Alcohollica, a bar in Marbella, Spain,
Metallica, a tour for the insane.
If fame were made of gold, I would melt it
And liquidate at market price, London closing.
If time was timeless, eternity would be now.
If space was only void, the universe would be crowded.
The loudest cry is that of a lizard
Who can't communicate to his sister.
My questions remained unanswered,
At least to my conscious state,
What of my love?
As I let go, they too will come.